`2017

specially for:
Erin M. Rose Walker
this book might be small
but it's powerful!
Enjoy your future goals...
with all our love,
and support.

Grandma, uncle Jamar, Jaliyah,
and uncle Alex.

Reaching Your Goals

Robin L. Silverman

Franklin Watts
A Division of Scholastic Inc.
New York • Toronto • London • Auckland • Sydney
Mexico City • New Delhi • Hong Kong
Danbury, Connecticut

Dedication

To Steve
With endless love and gratitude for the
many goals we have gotten together.

Cover design by Robert O'Brien.
Interior design by Kathleen Santini.

Library of Congress Cataloging-in-Publication Data

Silverman, Robin Landew.
   Reaching your goals / Robin Silverman.
      p. cm. — (Life balance)
Summary: Examines how to use imagination, thought, determination, and other abilities to transform a wish into a goal, visualize
achieving it, plan how to reach it, and ultimately find success.
Includes bibliographical references and index.
   ISBN 0-531-12342-1 (lib. bdg.)   0-531-16691-0 (pbk.)
   1. Goal (Psychology)—Juvenile literature. 2. Planning—Juvenile
literature. [1. Goal (Psychology). 2. Success] I. Title. II. Series.
   BF505.G6S57 2003
   153.8—dc22
                                    2003014720

Table of Contents

One

Imagine That!

"I wish I could be the fastest runner on the track team," Emily said. "I've dreamed about it again and again. I'm at the state meet, and it's the final lap of the last race. There are thousands of people in the stands, including my parents and my little brother. They're all cheering and yelling, 'Go, Emily!' I'm out in front, not by much, and my heart is pounding. I'm drenched in sweat, and I can taste the saltiness in my mouth. But the air on my face feels cool, and I can see the finish line clearly. I put all the power I have into my legs, throw out my chest, open my arms, and see my foot cross the white line just one second before the girl next to me. Then, over the loudspeaker, I hear the announcer say, 'And the winner is… Emily!'"

Have you ever made a wish? You know—the kind that burns so brightly in your heart that you feel as if it were already true. You can almost see, hear, smell, touch, and even taste what you want, even though nothing has happened yet. Wishes reflect who we want to be, what we want to do, and what we hope to have. Can your wishes come true? The answer is yes, if you learn to set and get your goals.

A goal transforms a wish from simply being a feeling in your heart to something that you actually experience. By imagining your wish coming true and taking well-planned action, you'll discover that when you put your mind, body, and spirit into what you want, it's easy and fun to get your goals.

It *Can* Happen to You

Jarrett and Georgia are two students who decided to be goal-getters. They were part of a focus group of ten middle-school students who tried a twenty-one-day goal-getting experiment using the techniques you'll find in this book. Behavioral psychologists (professionals who specialize in human behavior) say that it takes 21 days to establish a new habit, but more than 100 days of practicing it before it becomes automatic. You may choose any length of time to achieve your goals, but as you'll see, the more specific you are with your deadlines, the better your goal getting will work.

The ten students in the focus group included Mark, who wanted to exercise more; Tyler, who wanted to turn in all of his homework on time; Kayleen, who, like Georgia, wanted to eat healthfully and exercise more; Shannon, who wanted to have a better attitude; Megan, who wanted to stop biting her nails; and Annie, Ty, and Josie, who wanted to improve their grades in science. You'll hear what everyone in the group had to say about the goal-getting process through quotations in each chapter.

Jarrett's goal was to get a B or better in his science class, where he was currently averaging a D. First, he increased his participation in class. The more he listened and spoke, the more he learned. Finding more time to study was a little harder, as his friends wanted him to do things with them whenever he had free time. "Friends are a big distraction," he says. "When you go off with them, you think you'll have time to get your homework done later, but you don't." He learned to get his work done before he took time out for fun.

Jarrett changed in other ways too. "I always used to put things off and then try to cram in the information," he says. Now he began doing his work consistently. He turned in his homework on time. His effort paid off. Within twenty-one days, he had raised his grade to a B. "I'm pretty proud of what I did," he says. "And it probably wouldn't have happened if I just said, 'I'll try.'"

Georgia wanted to take charge of her body and her diet. She used the 21 days to establish some new, healthier eating and exercise habits. Her ultimate goal was to look and feel better, although she was pleasantly surprised that getting one goal had two unforeseen but welcome side effects. "The more I exercised, the more my grades went up," she says. "And I was also happier because I was eating healthier and exercising."

Georgia enlisted her mother's help. She decided to wake up at 5:30 A.M. to walk with her mom before breakfast. She also wore a wide rubber band around her wrist to help herself "snap back to attention" if she started eating the wrong things. Her friends decided to try the rubber-band technique too. (Note: If you decide to do this, make sure the rubber band isn't too tight on your wrist, or it will cut off your circulation.) "We got gel pens and decorated our rubber bands," she says. "My friends would snap mine against my wrist if they saw me eating the wrong thing."

By the end of the experiment, Georgia's body, grades, and spirit had all improved. Something else had changed inside her as well. "After I reached my goal, it made me realize I can help other people reach theirs," she says. "Now I can say, 'If you try, you can do it. If you tell yourself you can, then you can.'"

Just Imagine

Goal getting starts in our imagination. Imagination links our thoughts and feelings. When you think, you feel, and when you feel, you think. When something makes you feel uncomfortable, you think, "This could be better," and thoughts begin to gather in your head about changes. Or if you think a thought like "I'd like to know more about dolphins," you might get a feeling that leads you to do research on the Internet, in the library, or at a marine-biology center.

Our imaginations are so strong that we cannot stop them. For instance, notice what happens when you say to yourself, "Don't think about Katie!" You immediately picture Katie's

Feasting on Your Thoughts

Imagine a food you love. Picture it sitting on a table in front of you. What does it look like? What color and shape does it have? What does it smell like? Does it make a sound, like sizzling or steaming? What does it sound like as you chew it? Describe the taste and texture in as much detail as you can.

Check to see if you are salivating. Your body doesn't know that your thought isn't real. Just by thinking, you were able to set off reactions in your body that let you know if the food you were imagining is something you'd actually want to eat. (Imagine eating a raw lemon and see if you pucker up or get chills down your spine!)

face, voice, or behavior, even though you told your brain not to. This is because our minds are designed to create.

When you are goal getting, it's important to focus on what you want to get, not to eliminate what you don't want to have. Put your effort and energy into something you want to be *for,* not into something you are against. You want to feel good through the entire process. A little bit of fear or tension may be okay, especially if your goal is to get over something that's made you afraid in the past. Only you can decide.

Imagination can be used to help you build self-confidence and enthusiasm. Here are a few things you can do with it:

- "See" one of your wishes come true so that you can decide if you want to pursue it.
- Feel your way through a problem by imagining a solution and "trying it on" to see if it's right for you.
- Invent something brand-new by combining different images and ideas.
- Improve your relationships with your friends, family, and teachers by finding a comfortable feeling and seeing the images that result.

Choose Your Goal

Growing up, we learn what *not* to do so that we don't get ourselves in trouble. "Don't touch the hot pot!" "Don't go over there!" and "This isn't a good time" are examples of negative things we often hear. By the time we're eighteen years old, researchers say, we've heard the words "No!" or "Don't!" tens of thousands of times.

Although we are clear on what we're *not* supposed to do, it is much harder to decide what we *do* want to do. The first step in goal getting is to learn how to make choices that are good for you. Start by thinking about something you'd like to have, to be, or to do. It should be something you can control, not something like winning a color TV set in a store drawing or having someone fall in love with you. It should also be something in which you can achieve a result or see a positive change in twenty-one days. Some good examples are:

- getting a good grade on a test
- performing well artistically or athletically
- getting along better with a family member
- improving your diet or exercise routine
- getting rid of a bad habit, like watching too much TV
- creating a good habit, like studying for one hour each day
- meeting or getting to know someone better

To get your goal, remember:

- It must be specific. For example, the statement "I'd like to get an A in science class" is more specific than "I'd like to do better in school." You have to be able to see clearly in your imagination the result you want to achieve.

Make Your Choice

The reason that many people fail to set and achieve goals is because they give up. According to psychologist Steve Levinson, coauthor of the book *Following Through: Why We Can't, and How You Can*, there is no mechanism in the human brain for following through with them. In other words, once we've formed a desire about something we want, there is nothing in our bodies or brains to help us get it except good, old-fashioned determination and will power.

To make sure you're determined to get your goal, write down your answers to these questions on a separate piece of paper:

- What is one goal you've picked? Although you can have many goals, try working with just one first. After you have gotten this goal, it will be much easier to get others.
- Why did you choose it? Is it important to you or just to someone else?

- Why is this important to you right now? Will you be willing to work on it now and in the days ahead?
- Is your goal measurable? How will you know that you've reached it?
- Are you in control of whether or not you reach this goal, or is it dependent on forces or people you can't control?
- What does this goal say about you as a person? How will you feel about yourself when you're done?
- Who else besides you will benefit if this goal is achieved? If you can see advantages for people around you—like your teachers, parents, or friends—you'll be more likely to pursue it.
- How will you feel about yourself six months from now if you don't go after this goal?
- How will you feel about yourself six months from now if you do go after it?
- Do you believe this goal is possible for you to achieve in the time frame allotted?

- It must be something you believe is possible. Saying that your goal is to earn $1,000 for a new mountain bike by Friday probably won't work because, deep down, you know it's unrealistic. You have to feel confident that you can reach your goal, even if you're going to have to work hard or be patient to get it.
- It must be something you can measure. If your goal is to be happier, for instance, that's a goal that's difficult to measure. But if your goal is to laugh fifteen times a day, you can tell each day whether or not you've achieved your goal.
- It must be something you—not someone else—wants. Although your boyfriend might think that you should lose ten pounds, it shouldn't be your goal unless you want it for yourself.
- It must be something *you* can control. A goal of having your parents remarry after they've gotten a divorce isn't a good goal, because you have no control over their relationship. But a goal of spending an equal amount of time with each parent will probably work, as long as you have some say in the matter.
- It must be something you're willing to stick to. If you study like crazy and still get a C on a test, that doesn't necessarily mean that you've failed to get your goal. It just means that you have to keep trying or get assistance.

- It must be something with a reasonable timetable. A goal of trying to lose 50 pounds in 21 days is not reasonable and could hurt you, both physically and emotionally, if you tried to achieve it.

"Pick a goal you're willing to work for."
—Shannon

Throughout this book, you will see the term "goal getting." How is this different from "goal setting"? When you merely set goals, your thoughts center on the belief that there is a gap between where you are now and where you want to be. Although your goals might be perfect for you, if you believe that you presently lack what you want, your attention will automatically go to people and experiences that reinforce that feeling. It becomes self-fulfilling in a bad way. The more you think you don't have something, the more you won't—and the harder it will be to get it.

This book is designed to help you leap over that struggle. The techniques in the following chapters allow you to experience your goal as if it is happening right now. Every feature is designed to reinforce your belief that you already have exactly what you need to experience your goal not only in your mind but also in your life. As Henry Ford, the famous pioneer of the American automotive industry, once said, "Whether you think you can't or you can, you're right." So don't just set goals. Go get 'em!

Two

What Are You Thinking?

The human mind is very active. It never shuts down, not even when we sleep. In fact, the human mind thinks tens of thousands of thoughts every day. Unfortunately, four out of five of those thoughts are negative, not positive. We are constantly thinking of what we *can't* do, what *isn't* going right, what we *don't* want to happen, and what *won't* work.

Even people who try to have positive attitudes have negative thoughts. This is because these limiting thoughts serve three important functions. First, they're part of our survival instinct. Negative thoughts protect us every time we're faced with someone or something new that could potentially harm us or make us feel uncomfortable.

Second, negative thoughts are part of how we socialize. We are usually more jealous than excited when people tell us that their lives are perfect, thinking, "Why you and not me?" But if you ask a friend, "How are you?" and she responds, "I'm fine, but my day isn't going very well," you have a chance to bond with her as you offer your help or support. The negative provides something positive: a challenge for the two of you to share.

Third, we need negative thoughts because life would be boring without them. If everything were perfect, we would have nothing to do! So negative thoughts such as, "This isn't what I want" are actually quite useful. We can use them to set goals if we turn them around to "This is what I want instead."

Challenge the Negative

When Anthony was a teenager, he thought he wasn't worth anything. He had a learning disability that went undetected for years, and all his teachers and friends told him he was stupid. But one day, Ms. Soroka, the Resource Room teacher, told him, "You're not stupid, Anthony—you're just not organized. I'll help you get your work in order, and then you can do it."

The problem with negatives is that most people never challenge them. They believe change is impossible or will be too hard. They also use negative thoughts to explain away problems: "I couldn't get my homework done because I didn't bring my book home." Or they use negatives to shift blame from themselves to others: "I didn't do it. It must have been someone else."

Although a negative approach takes away risk, it also limits our growth. Try reading the sentences above out loud. How do they make you feel? Do you feel tight, tired, or restless? Negatives stop the flow of our energy, like a boulder in the middle of a path.

Now change the sentences. While some people simply say, "There's no way," others think, "What's the way past this?" Instead of "I couldn't get my homework done," try, "I didn't bring my book home, so I called my friend and borrowed his so that I could get my work done on time." Do you feel calmer, smarter, or more in control? Thinking this way can help you see how the thoughts and words we choose can make a difference in whether or not we get our goals.

This is what Ms. Soroka did for Anthony. She told him he could do the work, and she helped him get organized. As things started to improve, Anthony found himself saying, "I have a learning disability, but I can get help and do the work." He graduated from high school, got into a good college, and earned his first A. Soon he became a vice president of the National Honor Society and earned straight A's. Eventually he did so well that he received a full scholarship to law school.

Play with Positives

Try turning your own negative thoughts into positives. Using a separate sheet of paper, write down a positive alternative for each of the following statements:

- "Don't slam the door!"
- "You can't go in there!"
- "I can't do that."
- "This isn't what I want."
- "I don't want that to happen."
- "I won't be able to go."
- "I'm not ready."

As you make each statement above, pay attention to two things: (1) the picture that comes up in your mind, and (2) how you feel. Then try asking yourself the opposite: "What feeling do I want instead of this?"

Create sentences that make you feel happy and free. Instead of "I can't do my homework when the television is on," try "I can finish my homework and then watch television" or "I can tape my favorite shows and watch them later." Think about what you can do and how you might be able to get what you want. You may not always be able to control your circumstances, but you are the only one in charge of what you think or feel. So even if you can't stay out past 11:00 P.M. because of a curfew, you can decide not to get annoyed or angry about it.

What you've been saying to yourself may be keeping you from reaching your goals. Change what you think and say, and you'll discover that it's easy to get the goals you want.

Three

Who Do You
Want to Be?

There are two types of goals: short term and long term. Long-term goals are things in the distant future, like your choice of career. Short-term goals are things you can experience within days, weeks, or a few months. The best short-term goals contribute to the success of your long-term goals. For example, having a short-term goal of getting an A on your science test makes it easier for you to get the grades that will empower your long-term goal of being accepted into the college of your choice.

Selecting long-term and short-term goals sounds easy, but for most people, it isn't. Our attention is naturally drawn to what bothers or upsets us, rather than to what could make us happy. So if you accidentally hit your thumb with a hammer while pounding in a nail, the fact that your heart is working perfectly at that moment isn't going to matter. All your attention will be drawn to your thumb, where you're experiencing pain.

We can usually be specific about our problems, but happiness is a tougher target to hit. If someone asked you right now, "What bothers you?" you could probably list several specific things. But if the question were "What would make you happy?" you'd probably talk about getting rid of the things you don't want rather than describing one thing you enjoy and want to keep. The more specific you can be about what you like and why, the easier it is to decide the goals you'd like to get, which ultimately determine who you become.

How Do You See Yourself?

Every time something happens to us, we get to make a choice. For instance, when something bad happens, we can decide whether we will or won't start acting like a victim. We can try to get everyone to feel sorry for us, or we can be angry and bitter, trying to find someone or something to blame. Or we can choose to act like a victor and say, "Something bad happened, but I can use what I've learned to make things better than ever." Reaching your goals depends on how you see yourself, so the more you see yourself as confident and in control, the easier goal getting becomes.

> *"Even if you have low self-esteem, tell your-self that you can do this. After you get used to achieving your goals, you'll have higher self-esteem."*
>
> *—Josie*

Successful goal getting depends on your character and values. Character is the part of you that shows the world who you are, in both good times and bad. It is more than your personality. It's made up of the things you can't see until you speak or take action, like your ideas, feelings, conscience, and intuition. Character is who you are deep down, which is revealed in your relationships and experiences.

Taryn was a popular girl who attended a small, rural high school. She had lots of friends, a family who loved her, excellent grades, and a spot on the cheerleading team. One day she received a vicious e-mail message from someone she didn't know. It threatened her with harm, so she asked her mother to respond. Taryn's mother warned the sender to never send another note or else the family would call the police.

But the sender continued e-mailing horrible, scary messages. Each was worse than the one before. Taryn's father

What's Inside You?

Character qualities come from our values, or what we think is important. Take a look at the list below and see how many of these character qualities you have. Write them down on a separate piece of paper. Make two lists: one for the qualities you know you have and have already used in your life, and the other for those you would like to develop or use in the future.

loyal	careful	helpful
dependable	happy	flexible
responsible	hard-working	friendly
funny	organized	creative
kind	understanding	volunteering
thoughtful	inspirational	patient
accepting	reliable	observant
inventive	detail oriented	attentive
confident	critical	instructive

cooperative	imaginative	good with money
generous	responsive	curious
dedicated	positive	trustworthy
gentle	motivated	decisive
adventurous	enthusiastic	sympathetic
honest	energetic	truthful
contented	methodical	outgoing

Now take your list of the character qualities you've already used, and think of the situations where you used them. Take the qualities you'd like to have in the future, and imagine how you might use them to get your goals. Discovering and using your best character qualities should make you feel good about yourself. Perhaps for the first time, you realize that you are not just letting life happen to you. Instead you're in the driver's seat, pointing straight toward the person you've always wanted to be.

called the police, who called the FBI. Eventually the sender was caught, but not before Taryn suffered some of the most frightening weeks of her life. She lost weight, and her grades dropped. She called her parents on her cell phone every half hour. She retreated to the safety of her own home whenever possible.

The sender turned out to be one of Taryn's best friends, who had done the stunt on a dare. Taryn was sad that one of her friends could be so mean and vicious. She was also embarrassed to be around the rest of her friends because they were in on the "joke."

Rather than feel sorry for herself or be mad at the world, Taryn reached deep to take advantage of some of her best character qualities. She decided to use her intelligence, caring, and commitment to create a brochure for teens on how to stay safe while surfing the Internet. She thought she might print up about a thousand copies, but when she asked local businesses to help pay for the printing, she ended up with enough money to print ten thousand.

Taryn distributed her brochures to schools in her region. Then one day, CBS News called, saying it was sending a news team to do a story on her. Suddenly Taryn was the most popular girl in school. She went from being the class outcast to being the ultimate insider, all because she chose to use her best character qualities to deal with this challenge.

Creating Character

As you can see, there are many types of character qualities, but they all have one thing in common: They reflect what you believe to be important. One of the ways to develop more of the character qualities you want is to engage the help of others. There are many people who can help you, including parents and teachers, family and friends, and clergy. You can also look for a mentor—a businessperson or another adult in your community whom you admire. You can also develop your character by paying attention to role models, people you may or may not know who exhibit attitudes and behaviors you like.

"It's fun to work with someone else."
—Ty

To use your character for goal getting, ask yourself what you value. What kind of qualities will you need? What would you like to be true about you, both during the goal-getting process and after? Choose the qualities that you know work best for you in achieving great things.

You can work on developing those qualities yourself simply by becoming more aware of what you are saying, thinking, and doing. For instance, let's say your goal is to stop yelling at your sister. Your mother asks you to walk your sister to school the following morning, but your sister takes a long time getting ready. Instead of yelling at her to hurry up, you decide to use the character quality of patience. You slow down and match her pace, and you discover that you feel a lot less stressed. Although it's only one instance, you've already gotten a piece of your goal.

As you choose the character qualities you want, make sure your thoughts, words, and actions match your choices. You might want to write your thoughts and experiences in a journal, where you can study them more objectively. By writing things down, you'll quickly be able to see where you

Affirm It

One way to reinforce your visualization is with affirmations. Affirmations are positive statements that help you think about your success. They begin with the words "I am now" or "I now have" and are followed by one or more words that relate to your goal. Some examples are: "I am now in great shape" and "I am now cheery and upbeat around my friends." At first, you may think, "This isn't true yet!" But by stating your affirmations out loud, you help convince yourself that you can be, have, or do what you most want. If you find yourself resisting these affirmations, reduce them to a single word or phrase, like "health" or "success in science." Then simply think about what the word or phrase means to you. This is an easy way to keep your goal in mind while you're working toward it.

are staying on or going off track. Your character qualities are the fuel that help you get your goals, so don't hold back. Go for the gold inside you!

After you've decided the qualities you'd like to develop, think of someone who already demonstrates them. Ask that person if you could work together on a project that would help you learn and express the character qualities you've chosen. If the character qualities are harder to define, like "happy" or "gentle," find a person who seems to embody these qualities, and watch and listen as he or she goes about their day. You can learn a lot by observing. Finally, if the character qualities you've chosen can be applied to a celebrity, you may or may not be able to communicate with him or her, but you can still use the celebrity's character qualities as a model to improve your own qualities. Make a list of what you like or admire about him or her, then ask yourself, "How would my goal getting improve if I acted like this?" Friends can be useful too—but remember that they are also still deciding who they want to be. They are likely, however, to try to be like you if they see your character choices working out well.

"Most of my friends didn't care to help me reach my goal. It was something I did for myself."
—Josie

Four

Transform Your Problems

Mark sat alone on the wooden bench by the 50-yard line, holding his football helmet between his knees and looking down on the ground, where the grass had worn away to mud. "I can't believe I missed that pass," he mumbled to no one but himself. "I totally blew it! Now everyone will think I'm a loser."

Angela stormed through the back door by the kitchen and slammed it hard. "I'm never talking to Courtney again!" she shouted to her mother. "She told everyone I liked David, and now he's so embarrassed that he won't even look at me."

Although it may seem as if Mark and Angela have unsolvable problems, the fact is that when it comes to goal getting, they are actually quite lucky. Both of them know absolutely, positively what they do *not* want. Setting goals after a negative experience works because we human beings make changes in our lives for only two key reasons: to avoid pain or to create pleasure. The instinct to avoid anything that causes us pain—like the frustration of missing a crucial pass in a football game or being embarrassed by your friends—is the stronger of the two reasons. We don't like things to be wrong in our lives, which makes us want to fix them right away. It's harder to get excited about getting goals when we believe that everything is currently all right.

> *"If you have something that you're struggling with or want to improve, goal setting is a good thing to do."*
> **—Mark**

Knowing what you don't want is a wonderful way to focus on what you *do* want. Mark never, ever again wants to miss or fumble the ball during an important game. To state this in the positive, Mark absolutely, positively knows that he wants to catch every critical pass that comes his way. The same is true for Angela. She now knows that she absolutely, positively doesn't want her secrets broadcast to all her friends. Or she might have decided that she absolutely, positively doesn't want anyone else doing her talking for her.

Either way, a clear, positive desire has arisen: "I want to be in charge of expressing my own feelings." Angela now knows that she has the goal of getting the confidence to say what she thinks and feels when *she* wants to.

By going through the "back door, " both Mark and Angela have made a first step toward creating positive goals. To get on the road to being more confident on the field, Mark can start thinking, "I can practice catching passes until I complete

> ## *"Having a goal helped me because it kept my mind on what I wanted."*
> ### *—Annie*

them every time." Angela can choose thoughts like, "I can tell David I'm sorry everyone's talking about us and that I hope we can be friends anyway."

Try This

Identify a problem in your community that you would like to help change. Is there a vacant lot that needs to be cleaned up? A new student at school who doesn't have any friends yet? An elderly neighbor who has difficulty shoveling her walk when it snows? Pick a problem where you are willing to try to make a positive difference. Invite other people to help you, including friends, family, neighbors, and other people in your community. Fix a problem, and enjoy new self-confidence and strength.

Making Gains in Times of Pain

Sometimes we fail or make mistakes. Other times, it feels as if life isn't fair. Even with good goals and strong character qualities, problems can occur. No matter what has happened, you can control one thing: yourself. Pay attention to your thinking, choice of words, and actions in response to any situation that bothers or upsets you. Keep your reactions and behavior in line with the goals you've set and the person you know you want to be.

Take a moment to review the exercise in the previous chapter, where you identified some of your values. Also review the goal you set for yourself in the first chapter. You will need all this information for the following exercise.

Using a separate piece of paper, transform your list of values into affirmations. Make each one start with the words "I am" or "I have." Some examples are: "I am loyal," "I am patient," and "I have the ability to teach others."

Next, make a list of all the things you can

think of that might go wrong on your way to reaching your goal. What if your basketball practice runs late and interferes with your study time? What if you want to spend more time with your dad, and he gets called out of town on business at the last minute? Write down as many "what if" statements as you can think of.

Now look at your affirmations, the "I am" and "I have" sentences you wrote earlier. Which ones apply to the "what ifs" you described above? Write them here, as "If" and "then I will remember." Here are some examples:

If	then I will remember
my dad gets called out of town,	*that I am confident, caring, and flexible, and we can spend time together another day.*
my basketball practice takes away study time,	*that I am dedicated and healthy and can wake up 30 minutes early to study.*

Making Gains in Times of Pain *(Continued)*

Every problem offers you the potential to use more of your skills, which will ultimately make it easier for you to get your goals. Listen to your thoughts and words, and write them down. It's important to take them out of your head and make them real. Problems that are left in our minds become worries, and those can be harder to change. Then, write down a problem you have or could have. Next to it, write down the opposite. Here's what Mark's paper looks like:

"I missed the pass."   "I caught the pass."

"I totally blew it!"   "I did it!"

"Now everyone will   "Everyone thinks I'm
think I'm a loser."   a winner."

Another way to turn a negative into a positive is by writing down the answer to the question "What can I do about it?" Here's what happens to Angela's problems when she does this:

"What can I say to Courtney to make her understand my feelings?" *("Courtney, I know you didn't mean to hurt me, but I was really embarrassed when you told everyone I liked David.")*

"What can I do to win David's trust?" *("David, I hope you believe me when I tell you that I didn't say anything to Courtney. She just figured it out. But I'm really sorry that you're embarrassed. I am too.")*

The answers might make you feel uneasy at first, but that's all right. Most people find it challenging to use problems constructively. Sometimes it's hard to imagine good things at a time when things are going wrong. Allow yourself to imagine that everything has worked out well. When you can see the result you want in your mind, these exercises will help you think, speak, and act in ways that get you to your goals. Remember that trouble passes, but the lessons we learn about ourselves stay with us forever.

Five

Happy Endings

Have you ever read a suspenseful book and peeked at the last page before you were done, just because you wanted to know how things would turn out? We like being sure of where we are going and how things will end once we get there. We want to be in control of what is happening to us. We all know, unfortunately, that life is not always that predictable.

There is a tool, however, that helps us get where we want to go. It's called visualization. A visualization is a mental motion picture, showing us something we want come alive. It's more than thinking; visualization allows us to internally experience a scene as if it's actually happening, including how things look, sound, smell, taste, and feel. A visualization seems real, although it's not… yet.

Visualization is a wonderful goal-getting tool because it allows us to mentally "try on" the result we think we want before we take action. It gives us the opportunity to see if something feels right and seems to work for everyone in-volved so we can have confidence in our choices and actions.

> *"You have nothing to lose by trying this, and you may have a lot to gain."*
> *—Megan*

Your Mind "Talks" to Your Body

Vanessa was sleeping over at her friend Jenny's house. "Let's watch a really scary movie," Jenny said as she popped a disc into the DVD player. As the movie progressed, Vanessa started to shiver. Her heart began racing, and her head was pounding. "Turn it off, Jen!" she screamed. "This is waaaaay too scary!"

Vanessa was safe at Jenny's house, but her body didn't know that. As her imagination started to place her in a scary situation like the one she was watching, her body started to protect her. Her heart rate sped up to give her plenty of blood and oxygen in her brain and muscles in case she needed to run away from possible harm. Body heat left her arms and legs and went straight to her torso, to her heart, lungs, and other major organs, so that she could stay alive if she had to flee. Her head started pounding as a reminder for her to get away from the situation. In other words, her body had an extreme physical reaction— not to actual danger but to the mere thought of danger.

This is true with other visualizations too. What we see in our minds, we feel in our bodies. Because thoughts stir our biological responses, we can actually feel what we're thinking. The more vivid or specific our thoughts, the more we feel them in our bodies. Visualization, done correctly, makes us feel happy, peaceful, or excited about something we want.

Visualize What You Want

People often write down the goal they want to visualize, including all the details that help bring the scene alive. Start by choosing your happy ending. If you want to stop biting your nails, for example, imagine a scene where you are looking at your hands and your nails are perfect. Imagine smelling the nail polish when you open the bottle. Imagine the color you are painting them. Imagine running the polish brush along smooth, even cuticles. Think about what room you're in, where you're sitting, what day of the week it is, and what time of day. Keep going until the scene starts to feel real.

Imagine This

Have you ever baked a cake from a recipe on a cake-mix box or in a cookbook with a picture? Then you already understand visualization. The picture on the box or in the book allowed you to see the finished product in your mind. You could probably smell the cake baking and taste the flavors and textures in your mouth. You could hear the "oohs!" and "ahhs!" of your family and feel the plates in your hand as you cut pieces and passed them around the table. Try this with something else you'd like to do. Draw a picture of the happy ending you want, including as many details as you can. Then put the picture where you'll see it every day. It will help you get your goal, because the more can "see" it, the easier it will be to achieve.

To help create a visualization you will enjoy, answer the questions below on a separate piece of paper. Remember, the more specific you are, the better. You may want to write in pencil, so you can change your answers anytime.

1. What do I want to happen in my life?
2. Where am I when this happens?
3. What are some of the objects I see in this place?
4. How does this room or place smell?
5. What sounds do I hear? Is anyone talking? What are they saying?

6. What am I wearing? How does it feel on my body?

7. Am I standing, sitting, or lying down? What am I doing?

8. Who or what else is here with me? What are they doing?

9. Am I touching or holding anything? What does it feel like?

10. What is a word that describes the mood of this scene?

"Make your goal something fun."
—Annie

Once you have the details written down, write one or two paragraphs where the scene comes alive, like Emily's story in chapter one. When you visualize, you do this in the present tense, as if it is happening right now. This is because our bodies feel what we're thinking right away, and they don't experience the visualization as something that will happen at some future point.

Here's an example. "I am sitting in biology class on Thursday, the day after the big test. Mr. Smith, my teacher, has a stack of papers in his hand, and is walking up and down the aisles putting them face down on the desks. Some of the kids smile when they turn theirs over. Others moan. When he puts mine down in front of me, I can feel butterflies in my stomach. I lift up the top corner and peek at my grade. It's a B+! I give a big sigh of relief and feel a huge smile spread across my face."

Direct Your Own Mind Movies

An effective visualization includes descriptive thoughts and phrases that engage all five of your senses: something you hear, something you see, something you smell, something you touch, and something you taste. The more real you make it, the better it works to keep you motivated and on track toward your goal. To see how well you do it now, take this short quiz:

1. Can you describe an object well enough that another person can guess what it is without your actually naming it?

    ____Yes   ____No   ____Sometimes

2. Do you talk in pictures when you speak, saying things like, "I'm out of time!" or "My skin was flaking like a pie crust after I was at the beach all day"?

    ____Yes   ____No   ____Sometimes

3. Do you tell your friends what they should be doing to solve their problems because you can clearly see in your own mind what would result?

    ____Yes   ____No   ____Sometimes

4. Have you ever decided not to do something because, in your mind, you could see your

parents yelling at you?

____Yes   ____No   ____Sometimes

5. When you eat, are you aware of the flavors and textures of your food?

____Yes   ____No   ____Sometimes

6. Can you name five sounds (not words) that you heard today? (Give yourself two points for every one you can do.)

   a._____

   b._____

   c._____

   d._____

   e._____

7. When your parents ask you how school was that day, are you able to give them details about a conversation you had or what you did?

____Yes   ____No   ____Sometimes

8. Can you describe your best friend in detail, noting something special about his or her appearance, something he or she always says, and how you feel when you are with that person?

____Yes   ____No   ____Kind of

9. If you've ever had something really good happen to you, can you tell what happened in detail,

Direct Your Own Mind Movies (Continued)

including how you felt?

____Yes   ____No   ____Kind of

10. If someone asked you to draw or piece together a picture of your happiness from photographs in a magazine, could you do it?

____Yes   ____No   ____Kind of

Scoring: Give yourself 10 points for each "Yes" answer, 5 for each "Sometimes" or "Kind of" answer, and 3 for each "No" answer. (Remember to score question #6 differently, according to the instructions.)

80–100 points: You're a mind-movie master!

50–79 points: You're on your way to mastering mind movies and can get there with a little practice.

30–49 points: You have mind movies, but you're not watching them. Try to pay more attention to what you see in your thoughts when you speak. Focus on what you're doing while you're doing it. Your confidence in making mind movies will grow as you do.

Sara's Mind Movie

Sara's fourteenth birthday was coming up in three months, and her parents offered to take her and fourteen of her friends to the community swimming pool for a party, followed by a big pizza party at home. Her goal was to lose ten pounds and firm up her thighs and arms before the big day. To give herself the motivation she needed to get her goal, she visualized the following scene:

> I am running down the sidewalk. I'm 2 miles from home, at the turnaround point where I normally head back to complete my 4-mile run. The sun is shining, and there isn't a cloud in the sky. I can see a mother walking her baby in a stroller up ahead and cars passing by. I hear birds chirping in the trees and kids playing.

I can smell someone barbecuing something, maybe hamburgers. I'm not hungry, as I just finished a strawberry protein drink earlier. My old shorts and my school T-shirt are clinging to me because I'm sweating so much, but it feels great when the breeze blows and cools me off. I can feel my muscles getting firmer each time my foot hits the ground, and I can feel my breathing all the way down to my gut. When I run, I feel like I'm flying! I love it; I always wanted to be in this kind of shape.

The final step is to give your visualization a title. Sara called hers simply "Sara Gets in Great Shape." The title doesn't need to be fancy or clever, just something that feels true and acceptable to you.

After you've written your mind movie, read it out loud to yourself. If you like it, share it with someone whom you

Watch It

If you need ideas for your mind movies, take some clues from real ones. Turn on the TV, go to the theater, or rent a video where the main character in the movie has a goal or problem similar to yours. Study the scenes where the problem is resolved and he or she gets the goal. Use similar details to bring your own mind movie to life.

know will support and encourage you, such as your parents or a counselor or teacher. Discuss with them what you see for yourself so that they can talk to you about it and cheer you on.

"It's not that hard to choose a short-term goal. Start slow. Then it gets easier and easier to get to a long-term goal."

—Megan

Remember that you are the director of your own mind movie. Like all good directors, you choose the script, the characters, the motivation, the action, the set, and the outcome. It's good to have opinions from those you respect, but ultimately, the choices you make and the consequences they produce are up to you.

Making Your Success
Plan

 ow that you know more about your goals and your strengths, it's time to decide when and how you can get what you want. To transform your choices from being mere thoughts and wishes into a real-life experience, you'll need to do some planning.

Each one of us gets twenty-four hours in a day and seven days in a week. That's a total of 168 hours a week. Although it sounds like a lot, many people, unfortunately, pack their schedules so tightly that they don't have enough time to pursue the things that would truly make them happy.

Your Time Is Valuable

Imagine that time is money and that you

have been given $168 to spend in one week. You'll need to budget and to spend it wisely in order to obtain everything that's important to you. How are you spending this "money" now? On a separate sheet of paper or on your computer, answer these questions:

1. How much time do you spend in school every week? Take the number of hours per day, and multiply by five. For example, if you are in school from 8:00 A.M. to 3:00 P.M. that would be $7.00 a day, or $35.00 a week. If your travel time is 15 minutes each way, that's an extra $.50 per day, or $2.50 per week, for a total of $37.50 (round up to $38.00 to allow for those days when the commute isn't perfect).

2. How much time do you spend in after-school activities? If you find that you don't get home until 5:00 P.M. or 6:00 P.M., that means you're spending $10.00 to $15.00 a week on after-school activities.

3. How much time do you spend studying or doing home-work every night? If it's 2 hours each night, Monday through Friday, you'll want to add another $10.00 to your time budget.

4. How much time do you spend eating meals outside of school? If it's 1 hour per day during the week and 2 hours on each weekend day, that would be a total of $9.00 you use regularly.

5. How much time do you spend doing chores around the house? If you spend 1 hour per day every day (including weekends), put another $7.00 on your list.

6. How much time do you spend watching television, listening to music, talking on the phone with your friends, surfing the Internet, or playing computer games? If you spend an average of 3 hours every day, your total would be $21.00 per week.

7. How much time do you spend on family activities? This includes conversations with your parents, baby-sitting family members, going to religious services, or having meals with your extended family. If you spend, for example, 30 minutes on weekdays and 1 hour each on Saturday and Sunday, add another $4.50 to your total.

8. How much time do you spend sleeping? If you sleep 7 hours during the school week but 9 hours on weekends, add another $53.00 to your list.

9. How much time do you spend taking care of yourself (e.g., taking showers, brushing your teeth, getting dressed, doing your hair, exercising, painting your fingernails, etc.)? If it's 1 hour per day, add another $7.00 to your list.

10. How much time do you spend with your friends? For example, if you spend from 1:00 P.M. to 5:00 P.M. on both Saturday and Sunday with your friends, add another $8.00 to your list.

11. How much time do you spend working? Not everyone works for pay, but if you regularly baby-sit, volunteer, or participate in some kind of club activity where you have responsibilities, note how much time you spend there each week.

How many "dollars" have you spent? Take the original $168 and subtract the total of what you spend every week. If you spend the amount of time described above, you'll have spent at least $172.50—$4.50 over budget! Many people find that they're trying to spend more time than actually exists in a week, which causes a lot of stress and frustration and makes it difficult to get new goals.

Overcoming Obstacles

What if you find that your time is taken up with circumstances where you don't have control? For example, what if your parents say that you have to baby-sit when you were planning to study? Don't try to fight obstacles or remove them. Simply go around them as if they were boulders in the middle of the road. In this instance, try keeping your little brother busy with something quiet and safe so that you can study.

"There are so many distractions when you're trying to reach a goal. I think I would have made my goal if I didn't have my CD player."
—Tyler

Finding the Time You Need

Make a list on a separate piece of paper of the steps involved in making your visualization come true. Next to each step, estimate the time you'll need to complete it.

Scott wanted to be on the school soccer team, but his parents wouldn't allow him to try out until his grades improved. His grades were fine in all subjects but math, where he had a C average. It was early March, and he wanted to bring up his grade to a high B before May 15, when tryouts for the next year's soccer team would be held. Here's the list that Scott made to get his goal:

- Study math book and do math problems for 1 hour every night (total: 5 hours).
- Get extra help after school from the teacher when I don't understand something (total: maybe 1 hour a week, if she's available).
- Ask my parents to quiz me before tests (total: 30 minutes every other week).
- Go over my class notes in study hall twice a week (no extra time needed).

Scott looked at his schedule and realized that the only "extra" time he could find was on weekends. So he chose to study from 9:00 A.M. to noon on Saturdays and from 7:00 P.M. to 9:00 P.M. on Sundays, so he'd have his days free. Then, because he didn't have time after school, he asked the teacher if she could meet him before school for 15 minutes for extra help. She agreed.

Once he made his list, Scott used visualization to imagine himself studying. He saw himself sitting at his desk by his bedroom window on a beautiful Saturday morning in spring. His math book was open in front of him, along with several papers that had a variety of equations done in pencil on them. There were eraser marks on the papers where he had made mistakes but also some problems that he had done perfectly the first time. There was an empty glass next to him that had been filled with icy cold milk. The room was quiet except for the chirping of a blue jay in the elm tree outside. He imagined himself stretching and smiling as he looked at the clock: almost noon. He could hear himself saying that he'd worked hard and now it was time to have fun with his friends.

Scott made tremendous progress by visualizing and then acting on the other items on his goal list. He knew he was on the right track, and he felt great about himself. By May 1, his grade was a high B, and he had a good chance of getting an A for the semester.

"If you use a journal, you can look back and say, 'If I did this three days in a row, I can do it again!' Just fake it until it becomes a habit."
—Shannon

Staying Focused

Even with the best-laid plans, getting goals isn't always easy. Sometimes we find that we haven't devoted enough time to do the things we need to reach the goal. Or we may discover that for every step forward in our progress, something goes wrong to pull us backward. Your plan isn't destroyed just because it's been challenged. Get back on track by rereading your visualization, so that you can remind yourself of how it feels to have your goal. Then look at the list of things you need to do, and choose just one you can do with the time available to you. Lastly, give yourself credit for staying true to your goal during a difficult time.

It's Your Turn

Now make your own list of things you need to learn or practice to bring your visualization to life. Decide where, how, and with whom you'll invest your time so that you get the best return for your effort. Look at your time budget to see where you might be overspending. Can you give up an hour of television time a day so you can rehearse with your band? Would you be willing to trade an hour of computer games to get some time to exercise?

Once you've made your decisions, write them down. Copy the day-planning pages (see pp. 62-63) on a separate

Make a Date with Your Goals

When you're working on setting goals, it's not enough to say, "I'm going to do it!" You'll need to know what you're going to do, how you plan to get it done, and, most important, when you're going to find time to do it. Think of this process as making a date with your own happiness.

Start by listing your usual daily (Monday–Friday) schedule. Make separate pages for Saturday and Sunday. If you do something for many hours at a time, like sleeping or going to school, just put a line through those hours, since they cannot be used for anything else. Make a copy of these pages to get started; if you're trying to reach a goal in one month, make thirty or thirty-one copies, one for each day of the month.

6 A.M.   _____

7 A.M.   _____

8 A.M.   _____

9 A.M.   _____

10 A.M.   _____

11 A.M. _____

Noon _____

1 P.M. _____

2 P.M. _____

3 P.M. _____

4 P.M. _____

5 P.M. _____

6 P.M. _____

7 P.M. _____

8 P.M. _____

9 P.M. _____

10 P.M. _____

11 P.M. _____

Midnight _____

1 A.M. _____

2 A.M. _____

3 A.M. _____

4 A.M. _____

5 A.M. _____

Put a star (∗) by any hour when you might find time for your goal pursuit.

Make a Date with Your Goals (*Continued*)

You'll probably notice that your weekday schedule is very different from your weekend schedule. If so, when do you have time on weekends to pursue the steps you outlined? If your schedule is packed, is there something you can give up or rearrange to give you the time you need? What? How will you do that?

Finally, do you still believe that you have both the desire and the time to achieve what you want? What must change if you are to succeed? By answering these questions, you'll soon see if you're ready, willing, and able to get your goal at this time.

"Make a list of all the times you have five or ten minutes. If you can work a little bit on your goal each time, you're more likely to keep going."

—Kayleen

piece of paper. Then fill it in, scheduling your goal-getting activities as you would any other commitment.

Getting a goal is like putting together a jigsaw puzzle, where the pieces fall into place one at a time. You won't go from being a C student to being an A student overnight, but every time you complete another homework assignment correctly or learn another fact in class, the puzzle is coming together. Start with small, easy changes, so you can achieve some early success. As you gain confidence, you'll find it easier to make bigger changes.

To keep yourself motivated, celebrate each small step. You may want to put a star next to the items on your list that you've achieved or put a nickel in a piggy bank whenever you spend time on your dream. Look beyond what is left to do to enjoy what you've already accomplished.

"Try to get your parents to constantly remind you of your goal."

—Josie

Seven

Get Started Today

Sean's goal was to practice his saxophone for an hour every day so that he could perform a solo in the spring concert. "I've tried goal setting and planning," Sean complained. "It all looks great on paper until it's time for me to put it in action. Just as I'm ready to go practice, my mom will tell me I have to watch my little brother, or one of my teachers will announce a quiz that requires twenty pages of reading that night and then I'm too tired to practice. I can't seem to get going toward my goal."

"I know what you mean," Karen replied. "I want to enter the state science fair. Even though my parents are supportive of the idea, they both work and need me to do

Taking Care of Yourself

Once you've begun getting your goal, you'll want to be at your personal best so you can enjoy both the process and the results. Here are a few things that will help you build the mental and physical energy you need:

- *Drink more water.* If your body is only 2 percent dehydrated, you will feel more tired than usual. Try to drink several large glasses of water every day.
- *Get enough sleep.* How much is enough? You should be able to awaken without an alarm clock and without feeling exhausted or groggy. If you find that you can hardly hold up your head in class, you're probably not getting enough sleep. Try to get in bed at the same time each night, preferably before 10:00 P.M.
- *Eat as well as you can.* Try to limit salty or sugary foods, particularly those that come in a can, a package, or a box. Although they may taste good, they provide you with very little nutrition and a lot of empty calories. Try to eat at least five different fruits and vegetables

each day. They provide not only water, but also nutrients to help your brain and body function well.

- *Spend your time with positive people.* Stay away from friends or others who make you feel bad about trying to achieve your goals. Give your time and attention to those who encourage you.

- *Stop worry when it arises.* If you find yourself getting worried, say your own name out loud: "David!" This will snap you out of your worries and bring you back into the moment, because nothing gets our attention faster than the sound of our own name.

- *Do what you can do.* When you're feeling overwhelmed, tell yourself, "I have a million things to do, but right now, I'm going to do this." Then take action.

- *Turn off the television.* The average American watches more than four hours of television a day. Whatever your viewing habits, reduce them by 25 percent or more, and watch how your energy soars.

things like mow the lawn or wash the dishes, so I haven't even started working on it yet."

It's not always easy to put even the best-laid plans into action. The older you get, the more responsibilities you are likely to have at home and at school. Before you say, "Why bother?" here are some ways to take that critical first step, even when the circumstances of your life seem to be holding you back.

First, stop thinking of your goal in terms of all or nothing. In other words, just because Karen had to take time to mow the lawn doesn't mean that she couldn't get started on her science project. The key lies in a simple phrase: "If… then." For example, Karen could say, "If I promise my dad I'll mow the lawn every Saturday morning, then I'll have my free time the rest of the week to work on my science project." Put your responsibilities into your schedule first, and you'll quickly see when and how you can start pursuing your goals.

Another idea is to ask yourself, "How can I do both of these things at the same time?" In Sean's case, he can still find a way to practice while watching his little brother. For example, he can invite his little brother to dance, sing, or play along with him. Or Sean could practice his saxophone outside while he watches his little brother play in the yard.

A third idea is to share your feelings and try to reach a compromise. Karen could sit down with her parents and say, "The state science fair is in two weeks, and entering it is really important to me. But I need to get started now. I'd like some-one else to mow the lawn for a couple of weeks. Would you be willing to do it now if I agree to do the laundry for two weeks once the science fair is over?"

Any Day Is a Good Day

There is time for everything we consider important, although sometimes we must give up something to get the thing we want. The more vivid the goal is in your mind, the more likely you are to figure out how to get started on it. Once you begin, you'll find it easier to keep going. Remember, though, that no one else but you is responsible for giving you what you want.

"Put your goal where you can see it every day."
—Shannon

Learning how to empower yourself by setting and reaching your goals is the adventure of a lifetime. Visualization, character building, affirmations, and day planning are great tools that will help you now and as an adult. Play and experiment with them, and soon you'll be saying, "I got my goal!"

"Goal setting helped me improve my lifestyle. My friends complain, but they don't do any-thing to change for the better."
—Kayleen

Glossary

achievement: a great deed accomplished by bold action

affirmation: a positive, spoken idea that you believe to be true

biological: the nature of living things, including people

character: a pattern of personal behavior that reflects a person's values and morals

choreograph: plan the movements of a dance or an action

circumstance: the situation surrounding a particular event

compromise: a settlement between two or more people in which each side gives up something

mentor: a person of experience who gives you advice, encouragement, and possibly support in getting your goals

self-conscious: being awkward or embarrassed around others

self-esteem: believing in and having respect for yourself

visualization: forming a mental image of a situation, especially as you would like it to be

Further Resources

Books and Articles

Bachel, Beverly K. *What Do You Really Want? How to Set a Goal and Go for It!* Minneapolis: Free Spirit Publishing, 2001.

Covey, Sean. *The 7 Habits of Highly Effective Teens.* New York: Simon and Schuster, 1998.

Freeman, Lisa Lee. "No More Limits: Tap into Your Power with This Outward Bound Challenge." *CosmoGirl,* June/July 2003, p. 156.

Globus, Sheila. "Mastering Motivation: Whether You Want to Make the Track Team or Ace Your SAT, Motivation Is the Key to Making It Happen." *Current Health 2,* January 2003, p. 30.

Hugel, Bob. "Sisqo Sets Goals! R and B Artist and Actor Sisqo Hits the Right Notes When It Comes to Getting What He Wants." *Scholastic Choices,* October 2001, p. 28

Many, Christine. "Goal Rush: When Exercise Becomes Routine, It's Time to Set Some Goals." *Sports Illustrated for Women,* July 2001, p. 64.

McGraw, Jay. *Life Strategies for Teens.* New York: Fireside, 2000.

Online sites

www.mygoals.com
Offers goal-setting tips and articles, and a free newsletter. Gives specific suggestions and ideas for goal setting in hundreds of personal development categories. It is a great place to start if you don't know what your goal is or what it should be.

www.about-goal-setting.com
Gives a free goal-setting blueprint containing seven important steps to success.

www.topachievement.com
Posts a personal achievement quote of the day. Great article on Power Words, an alternative to affirmations. Includes discussion boards and a free newsletter.

www.gems4friends.com/goals
This Web site contains affirmations, general tips for staying healthy, and inspirational quotes.

Index

About the Author

Robin L. Silverman is an author and public speaker who shows men, women, and students how to use the mind/body powers they have to get the results they want. Her books include *The Ten Gifts: Find the Personal Peace You've Always Wanted from The Ten Gifts You've Always Had; Something Wonderful Is About to Happen: True Stories of People Who Found Happiness in Unexpected Places; North Dakota;* and *A Bosnian Family.* Her work has also appeared in many national magazines and anthologies, including *Chicken Soup for the Soul.* She lives with her husband, photographer Steve Silverman, in Grand Forks, North Dakota.

Acknowledgments

This book was an act of love, sharing techniques and information that I know have produced wonders for thousands of adults. I am grateful to the people who have given me the opportunity to present it to students.

First, I'd like to thank my wonderful editor, Meredith DeSousa. Meredith, you took a bold step forward by introducing the mind/body connection to the science of goal setting. Thank you for your dedication to informing and strengthening young readers in every way you know how. I appreciate your commitment to excellence and your willingness to learn about new things, people, and places.

I'd like to thank Wendy Soule, the Prime Time teacher at South Middle School in Grand Forks, North Dakota, who allowed me to work with a focus group of her students and assisted me. I'm also grateful to Nancy Dutot, principal of South Middle School, for opening the door to the focus-group project and making it possible.

To Jarrett, Megan, Georgia, Ty, Annie, Josie, Kayleen, Tyler, Mark, and Shannon—huge smiles and thanks. You are the best! I loved your enthusiasm, your energy, and, above all, your honesty. Thank you for your willingness to try the goal-getting process. I wish you all continued success.

Finally, I'd like to thank you, the reader, for looking at your life in a new and positive way. The world has more negativity than it needs, so every time someone says "Yes!" to something good in himself or herself, our planet becomes a slightly nicer place to live. I hope you will use the ideas in this and other resources to create a pattern of success in your life that gives you the confidence and resources to help someone else. If you learn how to raise yourself up, you'll never need to put anyone else down. You'll simply be able to lift him or her higher too. If just one reader does that deliberately, my hopes for this book will be realized.

I'd love to hear about your experiences using this material, so feel free to write to me: Robin L. Silverman, P.O. Box 13135, Grand Forks, ND 58208-3135.